FEATHERED FARM ANIMALS

DUCKS

by Elizabeth Andrews

Cody Koala
An Imprint of Pop!
popbooksonline.com

Hello! My name is Cody Koala

This book is filled with videos, puzzles, games, and more! Scan the QR codes* while you read, or visit the website below to make this book pop.

popbooksonline.com/duck

*Scanning QR codes requires a web-enabled smart device with a QR code reader app and a camera.

abdobooks.com
Published by Pop!, a division of ABDO, PO Box 398166, Minneapolis, Minnesota 55439.

Printed in the United States of America, North Mankato, Minnesota.
082025
012026

Cover Photo: Shutterstock Images
Interior Photos: Adobe Stock; Shutterstock Images; Getty Images
Editors: Tyler Gieseke and Grace Hansen
Series Designer: Julia Line

Library of Congress Control Number: 2025940516

Publisher's Cataloging-in-Publication Data
Names: Andrews, Elizabeth, author.
Title: Ducks / by Elizabeth Andrews
Description: Minneapolis, Minnesota : Pop!, 2026 | Series: Feathered farm animals | Includes online resources and index
Identifiers: ISBN 9781098248543 (lib. bdg.) | ISBN 9781098249069 (ebook)
Subjects: LCSH: Ducks--Juvenile literature. | Poultry--Juvenile literature. | Fowls--Juvenile literature. | Farm animals--Juvenile literature. | Animal husbandry--Juvenile literature.
Classification: DDC 636.597--dc23

Table of Contents

Chapter 1

Meet the Duck!

Ducks are birds. They live in groups called flocks. Female ducks are called hens. Male ducks are called drakes. **Domestic** ducks are raised for their meat, eggs, and feathers.

Watch a video here!

Ducks are covered in feathers. There are 17 **breeds** of domestic ducks. They come in many colors and sizes. The most common farm duck is the Pekin. It is white with an orange bill and feet.

Duck feathers can be used for stuffing and for fishing lures.

Ducks usually grow to be 20 inches (51 cm) long from head to tail. They are around 8 to 12 pounds (3.6–5.4 kg). Their feathers are covered in a special oil that makes them unaffected by water. Their feet are **webbed**.

Domestic ducks usually live 12 to 15 years.

bill

drake curl

wing

tail

webbed foot

Chapter 2

Life on the Farm

Farm ducks are calm. Many farmers let their ducks move freely on their farms during the day. At night, they sleep in **coops** to stay safe from **predators**.

Learn more here!

Hens start laying eggs when they are between five and six months old. Pekin ducks can lay 200 eggs a year. Duck eggs are larger and more colorful than chicken eggs.

Ducks need water. Some farmers put out plastic pools for their ducks. Other farmers have ponds and rivers on their land. Ducks spend time **preening** their feathers and looking for food.

Most **domestic** ducks are too heavy to fly.

Chapter 3

What Do They Eat?

Ducks eat insects, worms, weeds, and even small fish. Some farmers give them special **pellet** foods. Ducks flip upside down in water to find food.

Explore links here!

Chapter 4

Fluffy Ducklings

Baby ducks are called ducklings. They hatch from eggs by using their beaks to break the shell. Ducklings are covered in soft feathers called down. They can be many colors.

Farmers often keep ducklings under a heat lamp so they stay warm.

Ducklings stay close to their mother. They can swim when they are a few days old.

Ducklings lose their soft down feathers and **molt** at around six to seven weeks old.

Making Connections

Text-to-Self

What is one new thing that you learned about ducks from this book?

Text-to-Text

Have you read about any other farm animals? If so, how were those animals similar to or different from ducks?

Text-to-World

Ducks like to swim! What other birds like to swim? What else do those birds have in common with ducks?

Glossary

breed – a specific type of an animal that is raised by humans.

coop – a small enclosed space to house farm birds.

domestic – tame and raised by humans; not wild.

molt – to have old feathers fall out so new ones can take their place.

pellet – a small, round shape.

predator – an animal that lives by hunting and eating other animals.

preen – to clean, oil, and arrange the feathers.

webbed – having thin skin connecting the toes.

Index

Online Resources

popbooksonline.com

Thanks for reading this Cody Koala book!

This book is filled with videos, puzzles, games, and more! Scan the QR codes* while you read, or visit the website below to make this book pop.

popbooksonline.com/duck

*Scanning QR codes requires a web-enabled smart device with a QR code reader app and a camera.